# Romans in the
# Lake Counties

Dalesman
£1·25

WING OF COMMANDANT'S HOUSE,
HARDKNOTT FORT.

# Romans in the Lake Counties

by

**Tom Garlick**

With a Foreword by
Professor Eric Birley, F.B.A.

*Native god Cocidius from Bewcastle*

Dalesman Books
1976

THE DALESMAN PUBLISHING COMPANY LTD.,
Clapham (via Lancaster),
North Yorkshire.
First published 1970
2nd Edition 1972
3rd Edition 1976
ISBN: 0 85206 330 X

Printed and bound in Great Britain by
FRETWELL & BRIAN LTD.,
Silsden, Nr. Keighley, Yorkshire.

# Contents

# Illustrations

*Lakeland Photographic:* 2, 48, 49, 80. *Tullie House Museum, Carlisle:* 3, 17, 24, 29, 63, 65, 79. *Ministry of Public Buildings and Works:* 6, 72, 77. *Mansell Collection:* 10, 15, 26. *Museum of Antiquities, Newcastle-upon-Tyne:* 19, 35 (*bottom*), 77. *James Guilliam:* 21, 30, 34, 35 (*top*), 37, 53. *Dr. J. K. St. Joseph,* Cambridge: 23, 39, 41, 44, 55, 57, 58, 60, 62. *National Museum of Antiquities of Scotland, Edinburgh:* 31. *British Museum:* 32. *Map by E. Heeley. The photographs by Dr. St. Joseph are Crown Copyright reserved.*

A SECTION OF ALAN SORRELL'S
RECONSTRUCTION OF
HADRIAN'S WALL.

# *Foreword*

THE North of England is exceptionally rich in Roman remains. Hadrian's Wall and its associated works have inevitably attracted the lion's share of attention from archaeologists and antiquaries ever since the 16th century, yet Cumbria (to use a convenient term) has more Roman forts and Roman roads than are to be found east of the Pennines. For many years the Cumberland & Westmorland Antiquarian & Archaeological Society has paid careful attention to its share of the hinterland of Hadrian's Wall.

It is a matter for congratulation that Mr. Garlick has written such a useful survey of the evidence, embellished with a fine series of photographs and supplied with a detailed bibliography, in which the reader who cares to do so will be able to find fuller treatment of many of the monuments, mainly in the Cumberland & Westmorland Society's *Transactions*.

That Society's first Roman excavations were at Low Borrow Bridge. In the 1890s it carried out extensive work at Hardknott Castle, now in the custody of the Department of the Environment, each year more of its buildings being uncovered and consolidated for the public to visit. It was at Ambleside that the late Professor R. G. Collingwood did his most complete investigation of a Roman fort (now in the custody of the National Trust).

There remains a great deal more excavation to be done. It is hoped that the present guide will help to stimulate the interest which will encourage and support further work.

**Eric Birley.**

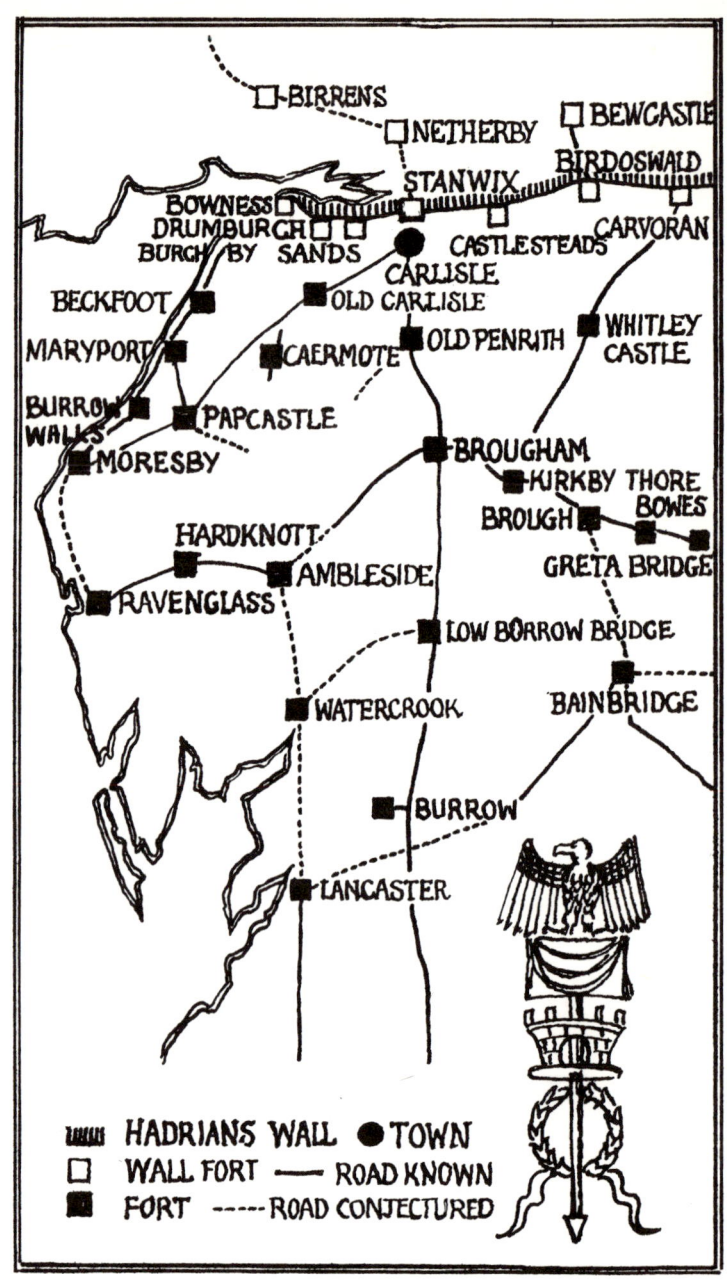

**A MAP OF THE LAKE COUNTIES
IN ROMAN TIMES.**

# An Introduction

W E have all heard of the Romans. Rome ruled Britain for nearly 400 years from the first to the fifth centuries AD — as long a period of time as separates us from the Age of Elizabeth I. In this book I have tried to examine the history of the Lake Counties of Northern England in Roman times, to describe what type of buildings the Roman army built here and to show what traces of Roman and Native the historically-minded traveller may find preserved in the area today.

The district we are concerned with was part of the military zone of Roman Britain, it lay in the frontier district behind Hadrian's Wall. This was a land of Roman forts and roads containing a native population who lived in scattered farms, hamlets and villages largely unaffected by Roman ways. There was only one Roman town, at Carlisle, but many Romanised villages (*vici*) outside the forts. I have also attempted by the use of archaeological evidence such as inscriptions, of which the area has yielded very many, to recreate what life was like for soldiers and civilians in the four centuries of Roman rule.

There are still many Roman remains to be seen in the Lake Counties, and they lie in some of the finest scenery in Britain. If this brief introduction persuades anybody unfamiliar with the period to read more widely about Roman Britain, to visit some of the sites mentioned and to follow the progress of archaeological research in the Lake Counties, its compilation will have been amply rewarded.

I am indebted to Eric Birley, until his retirement Professor of Archaeology at Durham University, who first stimulated my interest in Roman Britain, for reading and correcting my original typescript. He has kindly written a foreword. Such interest and enthusiasm as I have for the Romans, I owe to him.

9

The Emperor Vespasian, who devised the policy to subdue the North.

Trajan, in whose reign the first stone forts of Lakeland were built.

10

# Conquest and Occupation

ROMAN armies did not penetrate the Lake Counties of Cumberland, Westmorland and North-West Lancashire until the late first century AD. The Romans had invaded Southern England in 43 AD on the orders of the Emperor Claudius. Between 43 and 47 AD their armies over-ran the English lowlands. Faced then by hostile tribes in Wales and the Midlands Roman troops gradually annexed these areas too and by 70 AD the Emperor Vespasian ordered a completion of the conquest of Wales and an advance against the northern tribes; between 71 and 84 AD a series of energetic governors of Britain — Cerialis, Frontinus and Agricola — conquered most of North Britain.

Roman armies from the newly established Legionary Fortress at York may have first penetrated the Eden Valley of Cumberland, via the Stainmore Pass during the governorship of Petillius Cerialis (71 to 74 AD). Cerialis's orders were to invade and incorporate Brigantia into the Roman Province of Britannia. The Brigantes, the largest tribe in Northern England, inhabited the modern counties of Derbyshire, Yorkshire, Lancashire, Cumberland, Westmorland, Durham and Northumberland. Since the earlier Roman client-state alliance with this vast tribal area, established with its Queen Cartimandua, had broken down, her consort Venutius effected a palace revolution and assumed the leadership of the anti-Roman faction of the tribe. The result was war.

The Romans captured Venutius's northern stronghold at Stanwick near Richmond in 72 AD and then engaged in further battles with the tribe. The Roman marching camps identified at Rey Cross on Stainmore and at Plumpton Head, and Crackenthorpe beyond, probably mark the front line of Cerialis' troops in their strike towards Carlisle. No other

11

certain traces of Cerialis in the Lake Counties remain. He built no permanent forts and the detailed movements of his troops are unknown; it was campaign and partial conquest, not consolidation. Tacitus tells us that the Brigantes were crushed and large areas of their tribal territory annexed to Rome.

Frontinus, the next British Governor, was occupied in Wales from 74 to 78 AD and it was his successor, Gnaeus Julius Agricola, who built the first permanent forts and roads in our area. Agricola advanced with the 20th Legion and auxiliaries from Chester through NW England in 79 AD, passing up the Lancashire coast and moving through Westmorland towards Carlisle. Parallel columns traversed the east coast and links were established across the Pennines. This campaign took Roman armies up to the Tyne-Solway gap.

Tacitus, Agricola's biographer, remarks upon the skill of his son-in-law in selecting strategic sites for Roman forts, the intended bases for the garrisoning armies. As many of our forts were now built in turf and timber, none have certainly been identified in the central Lake District and it seems as if the Agricolan army by-passed this area in their northwards advance. The year 80 AD saw the Romans move into Scotland to the Forth-Clyde line and by 82 AD they were in South West Scotland contemplating intervention into Ireland. In 83 AD the Northern advance resumed beyond the Forth and the Roman army defeated the Scottish tribes in a great battle near Inverness in 84 AD.

Agricolas's governorship had seen a vast increase in Roman control over Northern Britain. Forts had been established at Lancaster, Burrow, Watercrook, Low Borrow Bridge, Brougham, Brough, Ravenglass, Old Penrith and Carlisle. Their construction with a network of linking roads was a considerable feat of military and manpower organization, and its achievement enables us to salute Agricola as the first Roman general to make a permanent impression on this part of Brigantia. Roman forts, established under him, continued to be occupied — with reconstructions and realignments — down to the late fourth century AD.

The older view that Agricola garrisoned the Lakes and contemplated his Irish expedition from the Cumberland coast seems untrue in the light of modern archaeological evidence. It was left to his successors to bring this mountainous left flank of the Brigantian realm with its forests, hills and mounttains, into the orbit of the Pax Romana. Under the Emperors Trajan (98 to 117 AD) and Hadrian (117 to 138 AD) Roman military control over this area increased, new forts were built at Ambleside, Hardknott and Ravenglass, and the period 100 to 110 AD also saw the rebuilding in stone of all the old Agricolan forts including the two base Legionary Fortresses at York and Chester. The Romans, consolidating their hold were here to stay.

But the Emperor Hadrian gave us our most impressive Roman remain—Hadrian's Wall. This was to be the Romans' final solution to the Northern frontier problem which had bedevilled their frontier policy since Agricola's recall in 85 AD. The Wall was the most elaborate defensive system ever devised to protect a part of the Roman Empire. Begun in the early 120s the new frontier was complete by Hadrian's death in 138. It consisted of a continuous stone and turf wall 80 Roman, $73\frac{1}{2}$ English miles long, running across the narrowest neck of England from the Tyne river to the Solway shore.

Set into the wall at regular intervals were forts, milecastles and turrets; behind was a protective earthwork, the *vallum*, and in the North-West three outpost forts. The turf of Hadrian's day, was replaced by stone during the second century. There were six Wall forts at Birdoswald. Castlesteads, Stanwix (Carlisle), Burgh-by-Sands, Drumburgh and Bowness; the western flank of the Wall, down the Cumberland coast to St Bees, being protected by four forts at Beckfoot, Maryport, Burrow Walls and Moresby and a system of patrol and signaling based on milefortlets and towers all along the shore. Roman control in the hinterland was strengthened too, implying suspicion of the local Brigantes as well as the Novantae of South-West Scotland.

Hadrianic occupation is attested at the forts of Lancaster, Burrow, Ambleside and Hardknott, but many Pennine forts were evacuated and their units sent northwards to help the Legions build the new frontier line. Hadrian died near Naples in 138. His successor, Antoninus Pius, ordered the re-occupation of Scotland and the construction of a second frontier wall between the Forth-Clyde estuaries—the Antonine Wall. Many of our forts were again evacuated and their troops sent into the Scottish lowlands to garrison forts and to man the new wall. Thus Hadrian's Wall went temporarily out of use.

The second century was the first full century of Roman occupation of the Lake Counties. By now all the stone forts had been built. The area, predominantly military in character, lay in the immediate hinterland of Hadrian's Wall and astride Brigantia and as such was vulnerable to attack from both Scottish tribes to the North and native Brigantes to the South.

13

Judging by the presence of 20 Roman forts in the area, creating a garrison of some 10,000 men, the Brigantian population must have been considerable, but it has left little archaeological record.

The Romans encouraged native farming to supply the needs of the Roman army for cereals, food and leather; the growth of Romanized villages (*vici*) outside fort encampments and extension of the Roman road system progressed. In the middle of the second century the Brigantes, perhaps profiting from the thinning out of Roman garrisons entailed by the occupation of Scotland, rose in revolt and attacked Roman installations. Antoninus Pius sent the Governor Gnaeus Julius Verus to suppress the revolts, Hadrian's Wall came back into commission and the Pennines were re-occupied. In the early 160s the next Emperor, Marcus Aurelius (161 to 180 AD) sent Sextus Calpurinius Agricola to continue the process.

Forts were re-occupied at Old Carlisle, Papcastle, Ravenglass, Hardknott, Ambleside, Lancaster, Burrow, Watercrook, Brougham, Kirkby Thore and Brough, but further trouble occurred in 169 and 175 and the century ended in turmoil. In 196 the British Governor Decimus Clodius Albinus withdrew many northern troops to fight his rival Septimius Severus for the principate in Gaul and the barbarians broke through Hadrian's Wall, devastating the hinterland. Many forts in the Lakes were damaged.

The Romans recovered Northern England in the third century. Severus emerged as sole Emperor after the Civil Wars and sent his Governors Lupus, Pudens and Senecio to evict the tribes, restore the Wall and rebuild the lost forts. Building inscriptions attest the restoration work of L.Virius Lupus and L.Alfenus Senecio at Birdoswald on the Wall and at Brough, Bowes and Greta Bridge on Stainmore. In 208 the Emperor arrived in person with the imperial family to lead a punitive war against the Scottish tribes; after battles against the Caledonians and Maeatae he died at York in 211, an old man wearied by his exertions.

It was under Severus that Britain was divided into two provinces—Superior and Inferior. Cumbria was in Lower Britain and governed from York. Severus also permitted Roman soldiers to marry on active service—an act that stimulated the growth of the fort villages. We have inscriptions datable to the reign of the next Emperor, Caracalla (211 to 217) from Old Penrith, Whitley Castle, Old Carlisle and to Severus Alexander (222 to 238) from Birdoswald and Old Penrith. In the reign of Postumus (259 to 268) there is mention of a newly created tribal unit, Civitas Carvetiorum, in the Eden valley possibly centred on Carlisle. Roman Carlisle was now an important town of 70 acres.

Further south, at Lancaster on the Lune, we have records of a bath building and cavalry drill hall built in the fort by the local cavalry regiment, the Ala Sebosiana. The closing decades of the century, which had been one of comparative peace, witnessed the onset of Saxon and Irish sea raids upon the province. In 286 the commander of the British fleet, Carausius,

The Emperor Severus.

made himself ruler of an independent Britain. His name occurs on a milestone found in the bed of the river Petteril near Carlisle It was Carausius and his successors who began to build a new series of powerful Roman forts around the British coast to protect the province from its new enemies; one was probably built at Lancaster, a hint that Irish raids upon the North-West had now become serious.

Allectus murdered Carausius in 293 and ruled briefly himself until 296. He withdrew troops from the North to fight his rival Constantius, sent in 296 by the Emperor Diocletian to restore Britain to the Central Government. The barbarians once more broke into our frontier district to damage the forts and Constantius overthrew Allectus, recovered the Wall and rebuilt the forts; he died at York in 306. By 305 Britain had been redivided into four provinces and Cumbria was now in Britannia Secunda.

The fourth century witnessed increasing disorders in the frontier areas. Picts, Scots from Ireland and Attacotti continued raids, culminating in the great invasion of 367 when the Wall defences broke under attack and the frontier forts went up in flames yet again. Emperor Valentinian sent Count Theodosius to Britain to restore Roman control and by 370 the Wall had been renovated and most of our forts rebuilt. A fifth province, Valentia, was created, with its capital probably at Carlisle. Many of the fort villages, sacked in 367, were not rebuilt and their civilians moved into the shelter of the patched up forts. The two late Roman signal posts, at Wreay Hall and Barrock Fell south of Carlisle, may date to the Theodosian reconstruction.

Peace was bought but not for long. In 383 a general in Britain, Magnus Maximus, withdrew troops from the north to fight for the throne. Many of our forts were evacuated but the Wall was still held. Maximus was defeated and killed in Northern Italy by Theodosius I in 388. Raids on Britain continued and in one such Patrick, son of a Roman official, was kidnapped by Irish pirates somewhere on the Cumberland coast. The Roman General Stilicho took steps to strengthen Britain's defences, but in 401-2 he was compelled to withdraw more troops for the defence of Italy. A final British usurper, Constantine III, withdrew the last remaining units in 407.

Thus by the early years of the fifth century all official Roman units had been withdrawn from the Lake District forts. The Wall too had been evacuated. In 410 the Emperor Honorius officially ordered the Romano-British inhabitants to supervise their own defences. There remained a large civilian population in the forts, spread out through the countryside and in those villages which had survived 367. Later Christian missionaries such as Patrick, Ninian and Kentigern found many people to convert in sub-Roman Cumbria and at forts like Brougham and Old Carlisle and at Carlisle itself civilized life went on.

Gradually, as the century wore on, the influx of invasions and the consequent decline in security destroyed organised Roman civilization. The Wall was never renovated and the forts behind it became derelict, used only as quarries or hermit cells. Future centuries saw new peoples invade our district— Angles, Scandinavians, Normans and Scots, each people bringing its own culture, monuments, place-names, castles and abbeys. The Romans faded into total obscurity and it was not until the reigns of Henry VIII and Elizabeth I that John Leland and William Camden, aided by many local informants, began to visit, describe and catalogue surviving Roman antiquities in the North-West.

Modern scientific archaeology has produced many aids, such as air photography, about which early antiquaries never dreamed. Today it is the archaeologist who must continue to unravel the story of the Romans in the Lake Counties.

Female pottery mask, a detail from a jug neck found at Burgh-by-Sands.

# *Roman Remains*

## Forts

THE *auxilia* of the Roman Imperial army were quartered in forts, small fortified camps of three to eight acres holding units of 500 or 1,000 men, in infantry and cavalry battalions. The legions, each 5,000 to 6,000 men, were accommodated in much larger 50 acre fortresses, of which there were only three in Britain—at Chester, York and Caerleon. Nearly 20 forts are known in the area of the Lake Counties. The first forts of turf and timber, some 10 of which have yielded pottery, were built during Agricola's governorship (78 to 84). Knowledge of what these early forts looked like has to be gained from comparison with other excavated examples in Britain, such as Fendoch in Perthshire.

In the Trajanic-Hadrianic period new rectangular stone forts were built to a symmetrical plan. These were of a playing card shape with rounded angles, stone-battlemented walls inset with four gates, and four corner towers. Outside the fort was a cordon of protective ditches. Within the fort the area was subdivided by streets, and a central area contained the commander's house (praetorium), headquarters building (principia) and granaries (horrea).

The commander's house accommodated the fort commander and was a fashionable Italian-style town house arranged round an open courtyard. It contained private rooms for the officer, his family and staff who enjoyed such luxuries as centrally heated rooms, frescoed walls and a private bath suite. The HQ was the fort's administrative centre, an oblong building entered from the fort's cross street, the *via principalis*. It contained two "L" shaped rooms or verandahs enclosing an open courtyard. Then came a covered cross hall for meetings and at the back the usual five administrative rooms for army paper work. The central room or *aedes* was the unit chapel containing the garrison's insignia, pay chests and symbols of Rome, the Eagle and a statue of the reigning Emperor.

Nearby were the fort granaries, housing supplies on raised flagged floors. The granary walls were heavily buttressed. The front (*praetentura*) and back (*retentura*) areas of the fort contained the troops' barracks, long narrow buildings with cubicles for the men and their kit, and a flat at the end for their officers. Other buildings included stables, stores and occasion-

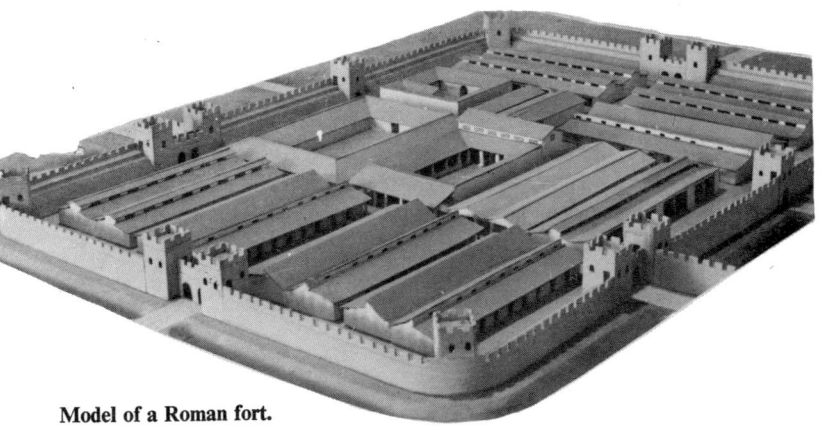

**Model of a Roman fort.**

ally a hospital. Behind the fort walls were cooking ovens, sheds and latrines.

Second and third century forts are noted for their regular systematic plan. Many in our district were continuously occupied from the late first to the late fourth centuries AD a period of over 300 years. Often damaged or destroyed in the wars of 197, 296 and 367, they were always rebuilt so that later forts covered the remains of the earlier ones. The grassy fort platforms we see today at Ambleside or Old Carlisle are the remains of these third and fourth century forts. A few like Hardknott were abandoned in the second century but the majority we know from pottery and inscriptions were held late into the fourth century.

Roman building inscriptions often give valuable information such as the name of the unit there, the type and date of buildings and the religious deities worshipped by the troops. The three northern counties have produced many important military inscriptions which have enabled historians to discover such details of Roman military life. Maryport and Birdoswald forts in Cumberland have yielded altars to Jupiter from their parade grounds.

Outside the fort walls lay not only the bath house and parade ground but also *vici* or villages, which tended to grow up outside most forts in the North and were inhabited by traders, civilians and, in the third century, by the soldiers' families. Some, like Kirkby Thore, developed into little townships. The best preserved forts in this area are the excavated examples at Birdoswald near Gilsland, on the Wall, and at Hardknott Castle near Boot, in Eskdale, Many are buried and invisible to the passer-by, as at Beckfoot and Papcastle in Cumberland, and Watercrook in Westmorland, but outlines of the buildings show up on aerial photographs. Some, like Old Carlisle, retain their rectangular fort platforms and one, Whitley Castle, still has a fine series of fort ditches.

The Romans controlled the Lake District by a network of roads with forts at the mouths of the main valley entrances into the hills. Further forts and signal stations protected the eastern approaches and forts in the North-West guarded the southern entrance to the area.

**Marching Camps**

The Roman army on campaign in enemy territory or on military exercises within the province also built temporary camps for the overnight accommodation of its troops. Their defences here consisted of earth banks crowned by timber pallisades in which there were four gates, protected by external projections. The camps, like forts, had straight sides and rounded corners and can easily be recognised on the ground if they have not been destroyed by ploughing. There are few known camps in the Lake Counties, Rey Cross on Stainmore, an 18 acre camp intended for a legion, being the best preserved of these. Two others of the same series have been identified at Plumpton Head and Crackenthorpe and three camps of varying sizes have been discovered near Troutbeck, Cumberland. Birdoswald fort on the Wall yielded fragments of leather tents of the type used by units in these camps.

**Signal Stations**

For lateral communication the Romans used beacon, smoke and semaphore signals. The Wall had tall square

Leahill turret (51b), on Hadrian's Wall.

Willowford East Turret (48a), near Birdoswald Fort.

stone turrets from which signals could be sent and the Cumberland coast had mile fortlets and free-standing towers down its length. Three signal posts stood on the Stainmore Pass, probably as part of a system connecting the Wall with York, and to the south of Carlisle the remains of two late Roman signal stations have been discovered.

## Roads

All the Roman forts in the area were connected by a road network. The construction of these new metalled roads with a cleared strip on either side, blazing a trail through the wooded landscape and over the bleak fells, must have made a vivid impression upon the native peoples, rather as modern motorways slicing through the countryside do on contemporaries. A glance at the road map will show the known main road network.

The main north-south route ran from Ribchester to Carlisle, skirting the Lake District, and receiving a branch road from York via Stainmore at Brougham. Roads from Carlisle led to the Cumberland plain. From Bowness, terminal fort of the Wall, a coastal road ran down via St. Bees to Ravenglass. In the interior of Cumberland the forts at Old Carlisle and Papcastle were important road centres and an obvious gap in the road system implies a lost fort at or near Keswick. Between Ravenglass and Ambleside an important route crossed Cumbria but no road is known further south through Furness, although a route across Morecambe Bay into Furness has been postulated.

The most spectacular routes in the area are those over Hardknott and Wrynose Passes, between the forts of Ravenglass and Ambleside, and High Street, a branch road that ran from the fort of Brougham to Ambleside, High Street accomplishes prodigious mountain climbing to over 2,000 feet with fine views of Ullswater. The total road network is not yet known but there has been much recent work done on it in Cumberland, especially into minor routes. Roman roads were once regularly equipped with milestones, but few have survived the centuries.

## Potteries

Roman tile and pottery kilns worked by auxiliaries have been excavated near Brampton and Ravenglass forts, while another site, worked by the local third century cavalry unit, is known at Quernmore near Lancaster. These afford valuable insight into the peaceful activities of the Roman army in the frontier zone. The Quernmore Kilns are now undergoing excavation.

## Native Sites

The native British population of the area in Roman times must have been large to justify such a strong garrison and the repeated revolts recorded by Roman writers. In the southern fringes of the district are the Iron Age hill forts of Ingleborough and Warton Crag near Carnforth. In Westmorland and the Western Dales were the farming settlements of the Brigantes which expanded under Roman rule.

The best known site is Ewe Close, a mile to the south west of Crosby Ravensworth village; a large nucleated settlement of hut groups, pounds and paddocks surviving still as earthworks

An air photograph of Ewe Close Native Settlement, Westmorland.

Model of conjectural restoration of Luguvalium (Roman Carlisle).

and associated with field systems—perhaps the village of a local tribal chief. Recent research has established that other native settlements spread over the Lune Valley, Furness and the Cumberland Plain. These villages changed little from those of prehistoric times and are wholly un-Roman in construction. They invariably consist of circular or rectangular huts with stone walls and thatched roofs; many invisible on the ground show up on air photographs and can then be examined by excavation. Their inhabitants exchanged agricultural products for Roman pottery but otherwise were little affected by the refinements of Roman civilization.

### Towns, Villas and Vici

The only Roman town in the area grew up at Carlisle (*Luguvalium*) which developed into a walled town of 70 acres; a typical Roman town with chequerboard street grid and public buildings such as a forum-basilica, baths, temples and town houses. We know something of its citizens from inscriptions and tombstones which came from the town cemeteries lining the approach roads. *Vici* or villages grew up outside the auxiliary forts on the Wall and in the hinterland, in some cases eventually covering a larger area than the fort itself, as at Kirkby Thore, where houses and streets can still be seen buried beneath the grass. Only one fort, Old Carlisle, has produced epigraphic evidence of a local village council with officials.

No Roman villa has yet been identified in the Lake counties. The nearest known are at Old Durham, Holme House (Piercebridge) and Gargrave near Skipton, in the West Riding of Yorkshire. These Romanised farms with their stone buildings, mosaic floors, frescoed walls and underfloor central heating are extremely rare in the northern military zone.

# Contemporary Life

IT is easy to picture in the mind the first tentative exploratory moves of the Roman army under Petillius Cerialis into this remote area of Brigantia, encamped on the wilds of Stainmore, its camp fires lighting the night sky, whereas of the subsequent campaigns between Romans and natives we know nothing. The later Agricolan army had to deal with the tribal groups of the North-West ensconced in their hill forts and villages; the period 78 to 84 AD witnessed great military activity in the area and we may imagine the raising of new Roman forts in fresh wood and new turves, the clearing of roadways through the wooded valleys and the ferrying of men, materials and supplies by sea from Chester. The local Brigantes were conscripted into the Roman army for service overseas and into labour corvees for fort and road building.

The second century saw the renewal of military activity in the stone rebuilding programme, the opening up of quarries for Hadrian's Wall, the extension of the Roman road system and the encouragement of native farming in the vicinity of forts. The Tyne-Solway gap assumed the character of a frontier with forts and fortlets connected by a cross road, the Stanegate, and the army built other new forts, one of these being on a ledge of Hardknott pass; it was completed in Hadrian's reign.

A visitor there today will have little difficulty in visualising Roman soldiers on duty, exercise and relaxation in this remote and beautiful valley. We can picture the military dress of Lakeland's Roman soldiers by analogy with Trajan's column in Rome, finished in 113, which shows a near contemporary Roman army fighting and building installations in Dacia — modern Romania.

AUXILIARY SOLDIERS AS PORTRAYED
ON TRAJAN'S COLUMN, ROME.

By the early 120s the roads of the Lake Counties were full of marching men and supply waggons heading northwards for the Tyne-Solway gap to build Hadrian's new Frontier Wall. We are told that gangs of soldiers sweated it out in the Roman quarries of Cumberland around Brampton, by rock inscriptions which have been found, and the Wall builders meticulously recorded their work on the centurial slabs set into the finished Wall. To the south the ditch diggers, by a prodigious amount of spade and basket work, carved the *vallum* behind the Wall. By 138 the isthmus had been walled off and the Brigantes separated from their compatriots and allies beyond the Wall. Down the Cumberland coast to St. Bees Head sentries, signallers and soldiers scanned the glistening expanses of the Irish sea for enemy shipping.

In subsequent Roman centuries, stone inscriptions found in the forts tell us about the life of these troops whose units were now strung out along the Wall and in the forts of the Cumberland mountains and the Pennines. They came from all parts of the Roman Empire—Gaul, Spain, Germany, the Balkans, Asia Minor, the Middle East and Africa. The 4th cohort of Dalmatians originally recruited in mountainous Yugoslavia manned the little fort on top of Hardknott Pass. At Lancaster in the third century a unit of bargemen was stationed on the Lune to negotiate the hazards of Morecambe Bay.

In the interior there was considerable economic exploitation. The garrison of Brampton Old Church fort on the Stânegate established a large tile and pottery works and, incidentally, buried some of their military scrap metal in a pit re-discovered in 1964 during alterations to a local school. At Parkhouse in Eskdale an auxiliary pottery was in production for the surrounding area. Lead was being mined near Alston and depots were established at Kirkby Thore and Brough forts.

Villages grew up outside many forts, their inhabitants attracted by the military market and its security. At Bowness-on-Solway a merchant paid for a shrine to the Mother Goddesses in anticipation of future profits. At Old Carlisle in the third century the villagers dedicated an altar to Jupiter and Vulcan on behalf of the Emperor Gordian III (238-244), it was paid for from village funds.

Civilian tombstones from the *vici* cemeteries tell us of a cosmopolitan population from all over the Roman Empire outside forts such as Burrow, Brough and Brougham. At Brougham in Westmorland, archaeologists have uncovered the civilian cemetery lining one of the fort's approach roads, consisting of simple cremation burials equipped for the after life with pottery food vessels and cheap trinkets. We also know a few personal names—Hermes from Commagene in distant Syria who died outside the fort of Brough, Flavius Martius, a senator or magistrate of the Carvetii tribe who died at Old Penrith, and six villagers from Brougham *vicus*, named Ressona, Audagus, Annamoris, Lunaris, Pluma and Baculo.

Surviving tombstones enable the Romanised dress of the civilians to be recreated. At Carlisle a rich Romano-British lady seated in a wicker cushioned chair, clasping her fan and lively offspring looks out at us from her tombstone and there is the effigy of little Vacia, aged three, in her belted overcoat, who died in the same city. Information on military dress is less profuse—the odd pieces of scale armour from a fort and fragments of Roman soldiers' shoes from Hardknott, Ambleside and Low Borrow Bridge. A relief from Old Carlisle shows the torso of an officer with his cloak, belt and sword.

Local peasants have left us less tangible memorials in the form of their scattered hut and field settlements. We can picture them mingling in the fort *vici* or at the fairs held under Roman authority, speaking their native Celtic but maintaining an independent custom and existence. They were the great silent majority of the Lake Counties in Roman Times, no doubt regularly visited by Roman tax collectors and officials thirsting for the Emperor's rights.

Roman fort gateway inscriptions in Latin, found at such forts at Moresby and Hardknott from Hadrian's reign, proclaimed in Roman monumental lettering the proud titles and victories of their Divine Majesties whose imperial sway had penetrated even these remote fell lands, and periodically the troops in forts like Old Carlisle expressed their corporate loyalty to the ruling house. At Lancaster the local unit put up a new cavalry exercise hall and baths. At Birdoswald fort and along the Stainmore Pass inscriptions tell us of forts recovered and rebuilt after damage by the enemy under the Emperors Severus and Diocletian; while along the straight metalled roads tall cylindrical milestones proclaimed the reigning Emperor and distance from the next Roman fort or town.

We can see, too, evidence of war. At Ambleside on Windermere a tombstone records a young soldier killed in the fort by the enemy. At Carlisle a prefect of a cavalry unit offers a dedication to Hercules, in the reign of Commodus, after the slaughter of a band of barbarians. At Kirksteads near Carlisle a Legate of the VI Legion records on his inscription successful military operations beyond the Wall. But there were also

CANOPIED TOMBSTONE c.2nd CENTURY,
FROM CARLISLE.

many decades of peace between the frontier wars. At Lancaster in the fertile fields about the flowing Lune, a retired officer from the nearby fort set up an altar to Ialonus, local god of the meadowland in thanks for peaceful farming.

We know a lot about the Roman army's religious beliefs too from epigraphy. In the moors about the Stainmore Pass soldiers dedicated two small shrines to Vinotonus and Silvanus, patron deities of hunting in the wilds. At Bewcastle the troops worshipped the local godling Cocidius and another favourite was Belatucadrus who occurs at many forts in Cumberland and Westmorland. At Maryport on the coast a whole series of Roman altars were found in pits buried around the fort's parade ground recording the worship of Jupiter and Mars and telling much about the officers who dedicated them. In late Roman times there is epigraphic evidence for the presence of Christians at Maryport, Carlisle, Brough and Bowes.

We have useful information on army signalling too from the Wall and along Stainmore. Southwards at Lancaster the new late Roman defensive architecture of the forts of the Saxon Shore has revealed itself—with high walls, mural towers, and narrow gates, the early ancestors of the medieval castle. At Birrens in Dumfriesshire, just outside Cumbria but within the Brigantian state, is a fine relief of Dea Brigantia, a personification of the goddess Brigantia herself. The figure of the goddess stands frontally in a gabled niche, wearing a cloak, a long tunic and turreted crown. She holds a shield and spear like Minerva, while from her shoulders spring wings of victory. In her right hand is a globe-emblem of the vast Brigantian realm of moor and mountain. Her dedicator Amandus was a Roman military architect and wrote in Latin. Here is a native goddess bedecked in Roman trappings.

**Harrow's Scar Milecastle near Birdoswald.**

**A DEDICATION TO THE GODDESS
BRIGANTIA FOUND AT BIRRENS.**

# Hadrian's Wall

THE western half of Hadrian's Wall runs through modern Cumberland. In Hadrian's day the wall, forts and milecastles were built of turf and timber with stone turrets but the whole thing was rebuilt in stone sometime in the second century. The western flank of the new frontier was lavishly protected by three outpost forts in the North-West, a thousand strong crack cavalry regiment at Stanwix, north of Carlisle and a system of forts and signal towers down the Cumberland coast. Visitors will need the *Roman Wall Handbook* and the Ordnance Survey Map of Hadrian's Wall if they intend to follow the remains.

The course of the Wall in Cumberland is relatively flat and unimpressive compared with the splendid stretch through central Northumberland. Here there were six wall forts at

**A Head of Emperor Hadrian recovered from the Thames.**

Birdoswald, Castlesteads, Stanwix, Burgh-by-Sands, Drum-burgh and Bowness. Tullie House museum in Carlisle contains a fine collection of Roman material from this Western sector. Birdoswald near Gilsland is the best preserved fort to visit because its walls have been excavated and exposed to public view. Carlisle or Brampton would make good centre bases for those intending a lengthy visit to the Wall. In this section I shall describe the chief visible remains the motorist or walker should try to see in Cumberland.

At Gilsland there are lengths of the Wall exposed in the former vicarage garden and two turrets 48a and 48b, in the curtain wall leading to the Roman bridge across the river Irthing at Willowford. Turrets were small square stone signal towers set into the south face of the wall at intervals of 540 yards. Only their foundations survive. From the single door-way at ground level, inside steps gave access to an upper storey, which could be entered from the Wall sentry walk too. Their tops were once flat and battlemented.

West of Gilsland railway station is a well preserved Mile-castle 48, Poltross Burn.

Milecastles were small fortlets every Roman mile along the Wall housing wall and *vallum* patrols. This one, excavated by F. G. Simpson in ·1909, was found to contain two troop barracks, a cooking oven and a staircase up to the Wall, it had two gates and rounded corners. Today diesel trains thunder past it between Newcastle and Carlisle. Returning to Gilsland we can follow the Wall down to Willowford Roman Bridge Abutment, in the fields by the farm. There was once a bridge here carrying the great Wall across the river Irthing. The Wall then climbed up the steep bank beyond to the site of Milecastle 49, Harrow's Scar.

There is a fine length of the Wall from the milecastle to the fort at Birdoswald. Notice the outer facings of the Wall made of squared stone blocks and the rubble fill. Originally the Wall stood some fifteen feet to the sentry walk. Birdoswald fort projects south of the Wall and is situated on a bluff above the Irthing, a modern farm occupying its North-West quarter. The visitor should walk round the defences and examine the fine east gateway with its double guard chambers, the fort's rounded angles and postern gate.

A short walk from the south gate leads to the edge of the escarpment overlooking the Irthing gorge. This view gave the fort its name—Camboglanna—"Crooked Glen", and in leafy summer one can look down at the river curving through the wooded glen, one of the most beautiful in Cumberland.

Hadrian's Wall as it survives at Gilsland. In the background is the former vicarage.

Left: Narrow Wall on broad foundation near Willowford Bridge.

**Right: View of the Irthing gorge from Birdoswald fort.**

**Model of a Turf Wall milecastle (50), west of Birdoswald fort.**

The interior of the fort is grass grown and cows graze where once the Headquarters, granaries and stables stood. It was at Birdoswald in 1929 that two important inscriptions were found mentioning the restoration of the fort under Severus and Diocletian at the start of Wall Period II (200 to 296) and Wall Period III (300 to 367). The fort has yielded nearly twenty altars to Jupiter Best and Greatest dedicated by successive officers of the Ist cohort of Dacians and found in pits around the fort parade ground. Featured in local lore as the site of King Arthur's last battle, Birdoswald fort has a quiet fascination about it.

About six miles northwards lies Bewcastle, site of the only Wall outpost fort to be seen in Cumberland. The other at Netherby is covered by a modern mansion and its ornamental grounds. The visible fort at Bewcastle is Severan, occupies a small hummock and is of an unusual hexagonal shape, unlike the regular plan of Wall forts. The south-east angle is occupied by a later castle and inside the fort, by the church, is the famous Bewcastle Cross, a symbol of the introduction of Christianity into these wild wastes.

From Birdoswald it is possible to follow the wall Westwards as it has been uncovered and consolidated by the Ministry. In this sector reference to the Ordnance Survey Map will show the lines of the Stone and Turf Walls. The Turf Wall, discovered in 1895, can be seen at Appletree. Further on is Banks East Turret, 52a, a turf wall turret later incorporated in the stone wall. To the south are the sites of several Stanegate Roman forts at Nether Denton, Castle Hill Boothby and Old Church Brampton. Lanercost priory, largely built of stones from the Roman Wall, is worth visiting as it has a small museum.

The next Wall fort is at Castlesteads, Uxellodunum, seven miles west of Birdoswald. It lies on a bluff above the Cambeck but there is nothing visible, since the fort was levelled in the late 18th century to make the gardens of Castlesteads House. Excavations in 1934 located the outlines of a $3\frac{1}{2}$ acre fort which was not attached to the Wall like Birdoswald, in a gap between the Wall and vallum.

The fort at Stanwix is covered by modern buildings and the parish church and churchyard. Its dimensions were only discovered in 1940. It accommodated a 1,000 cavalry unit and was called Petriana. The best place to visit next is Tullie House Museum at Carlisle, which has a fine Roman collection and then, using a map try to follow the course of the Wall out of the City to Bowness.

At Burgh-by-Sands a five acre cavalry fort (Aballava), lies

buried beneath part of the present village and churchyard. Leaving Burgh and proceeding via Dykesfield and Burgh Marsh, Drumburgh fort (Congavata) is reached. This two acre fort was looted in the 16th century to build a manor house.

Bowness-on-Solway (Maia) is the site of the last Wall fort and terminal point of Hadrian's Wall. The large seven acre fort faced westwards across the Solway and there was probably a village port here in Roman times. The Wall ran westwards from the north-west angle of the fort and ended in a turret some way along the cliffs. The coastline here is flat and un-interesting but across the Solway rise the hills of Scotland, home of the tribesmen who once threatened the boundless majesty of the Roman Peace.

Westwards at Cardurnock, the chain of mile fortlets and signal towers, which carried the Wall defences for another 40 miles down the Cumberland coast begins. The Wall itself terminated at Bowness, this being the lowest point at which the Solway can be forded. Down the coast are four more forts which lent military support for the coastal patrols.

**East gate at Birdoswald fort, Hadrian's Wall.**

# Cumberland Coastal Defences

A SYSTEM of four forts, milefortlets and watch towers protected the left flank of Hadrian's Wall down to St. Bees. This system corresponds to the fort, milecastle, turret sequence on the Wall but here there was no curtain wall. The Romans treated the Cumberland coast like the European rivers of the Rhine and Danube, providing its bank with camps and signal posts for the spotting and interception of raiders, the Novantae of South-West Scotland and perhaps the Irish. The elucidation of this system of watching and patrol has been due to Mr. R. L. Bellhouse whose reports appear regularly in the *Transactions of the Cumberland and Westmorland Antiquarian and Archaeological Society*.

The milefortlets were small patrol posts within turf ramparts protected by a ditch and they show up clearly on air photographs. The watchtowers were free standing stone towers, two between each pair of mile fortlets. They occur every 540 yards and had an internal staircase giving access to a flat look-out platform on the top. Hadrian equipped the system with four cohort forts at Beckfoot, Maryport, Burrow Walls and Moresby.

### Beckfoot.

Beckfoot fort (Bibra) lies ten miles south of Bowness. The site can be reached along B5300 Silloth to Allonby road. The 3 acre fort, now buried, was south of Beckfoot farm facing seawards and was not discovered until 1879. Its walls, gates and internal buildings show up under the grass on a spectacular air photograph taken by Dr. K. St. Joseph in 1949. Its garrison in the second century was the second cohort of Lingones. It had a *vicus*, and pottery shows an occupation well into the 4th century.

BECKFOOT FORT
PHOTOGRAPHED FROM THE AIR.

## Maryport.

Maryport Roman fort stands on a hill north of the river Ellen in a field beyond the market place by the sea. Its Roman name was Alauna. The fort platform is clear and early antiquaries recorded the area as being littered with Roman remains. Stukeley mentions traces of the *vicus* and the fine views to Scotland and the Isle of Man from this $5\frac{3}{4}$ acre fort which, like the others, faced seawards. A port existed down by the river Ellen as Alauna was an important supply base for Cumberland and Roman campaigns in Scotland.

A fine series of Roman altars, found outside the fort parade ground in the late 19th century, offer successive dedications to Jupiter by the local garrison. The altars came from pits around the parade ground and represent the Roman army's regular renewal of vows for the Emperors' health and safety on his birthday and on January 3, when new altars were erected and the old ones ceremonially buried. The altars also record the fort garrisons—cohort I Hispanorum under Hadrian; cohort I Delmatarum under Pius. and later in the second century, cohort I Baetasiorum. The first fort on the site may have been Agricolan with a stone fort built later under Trajan or Hadrian. The site which was occupied well into the fifth century, has yielded a Chi-Rho monogram attesting Christians.

The fort was connected by road down the coast and into the interior of Cumberland. The visitor should not miss seeing the fine Roman inscriptions collected by the Senhouse family since Tudor times at Netherhall Lodge. It is to be hoped they will some day become part of a site museum which would be a fitting tribute to the numerous antiquaries and archaeologists who have worked down the centuries since Camden's day to record and investigate this important Roman site.

## Burrow Walls.

Five miles south of Maryport on the outskirts of Workington lies the site of Burrow Walls fort (Gabrosentum), buried in fields overlooking the river Derwent. It was not discovered until 1955 by which time its western half had been destroyed by sea erosion. Pottery discovered there implies an occupation under Hadrian, renewed in the fourth century. Returning to Workington, the A596 Whitehaven road leads to the last fort in the Hadrianic coastal defences, at Moresby.

**Moresby.**

This site can be seen from the road near the turn off down to Parton village. The present church of St. Bridget's lies inside the fort platform which is clear and is in part covered by the churchyard. In 1822, the local vicar discovered a Hadrianic building inscription from the fort's east gate. Its Roman name was Tunnocelum. Today a sewerage works lies below it and there is a towering colliery tip, while from the windswept churchyard the whole coastline can be seen as far as Whitehaven, a busy little West Cumberland town. The next fort past St. Bees was at Ravenglass which faced up Eskdale and turned its back on the sea.

**Maryport Roman fort as seen from the air.**

# The Cumberland Plain

THE Cumberland Plain was densely studded with native farms but had no known villa. There was one Roman town at Carlisle and three forts—at Old Carlisle, Caermote and Papcastle.

**Carlisle.**

Roman Carlisle began as a Cerealian camp or an Agricolan fort. On its northern outskirts was later built the wall fort of Stanwix. Carlisle became a Roman town, Luguvalium, behind the frontier but an important road centre. It was not the tribal capital of the Brigantes, which lay at Aldborough near Boroughbridge but this 70 acre town acquired administrative importance in late Roman times.

The Roman town is buried below its medieval and modern successors, but selective excavations and finds in the City tell us something about it. It acquired the usual Roman street grid and public buildings. In the third century it was walled and was the market centre of the Cumberland Plain. The major finds can be seen in Tullie House Museum.

One of its inhabitants, a Greek called Papias, was probably a Christian, and in sub-Roman times it may have acquired a bishop. As late as 685 its Anglian inhabitants proudly showed Cuthbert, Bishop of Lindisfarne, the ruins of the old Roman town walls and a Roman fountain.

**Native sites.**

Recent work has established the existence of many native settlements in the vicinity of the forts at Beckfoot, Maryport, Old Carlisle and Old Penrith. There was considerable expansion of local farming to meet the needs of the Romans. Sites such as Wolsty Hall, north of Beckfoot, show clearly on air photographs. Their inhabitants lived in circular huts within pounds, and used Roman pottery, and followed Roman roads to market their produce. Otherwise they were only affected by the thinnest veneer of Romanisation. They in turn benefited from the security of the forts and their markets.

### Old Carlisle.

The Roman fort at Old Carlisle was called Olenacum. It lies a mile south of Wigton, being located in a field by the road overlooking the Wiza beck. Its fort platform is clearly visible and air photographs show a large *vicus*. Camden visited it in 1599 and Stukeley called during his rounds of 1725, telling us that the *vicus* was still visible. Horsley included a plan of the site in his *Britannia Romana* (1732).

Old Carlisle was a large cavalry fort whose commander was the senior officer in West Cumberland south of the Wall. The fort has yielded many inscriptions, and one of them, found in 1842, mentions a village council. The fort was a road hub with routes to the Wall, Carlisle, Old Penrith, and Papcastle. It was occupied from Hadrian's reign until the late fourth century, and perhaps into sub-Roman times. Later the fort was used as a quarry for the local church and farms. Several native sites are known S.W. of the fort near the Roman roads, and they might have produced food for the Roman garrison.

### Caermote.

Caermote, often overlooked, is a Roman fort site near Bothel. West first records Roman remains there in his *Guide to the Lakes* (1778). Two turf forts are visible, a $3\frac{1}{2}$ acre cohort camp and within its N.W. corner a smaller fortlet. The fort's function may have been to guard the lead mining area of Caldbeck and to act as its depot. Precise dating of the two forts is uncertain.

The site is reached by following A591 from Keswick, N. of Bassenthwaite lake to just beyond Bewaldeth village.

### Papcastle.

Papcastle, a small village across the Derwent from Cockermouth, had the Roman fort of Derventio, which now lies buried in fields. Stukeley visited the fort in 1725, mentioning a large *vicus* outside the establishment, and Collingwood excavated in the fort in 1922, discovering part of the defences.

An aerial photograph of 1954 shows the fort walls and west gate.

Excavations by Miss Dorothy Charlesworth in 1961/2 unearthed traces of the barrack blocks and the commander's baths relating to a fourth century fort, which was large, of $6\frac{3}{4}$ acres, housing a cavalry unit.

Papcastle was a road centre, like Old Carlisle, the garrison here kept watch on the Cumbrian Fells and guarded the route southwards to Ravenglass. Its place name may be derived from the Old Norse "Papi" a hermit, suggesting that Scandinavian invaders found a hermit's lodge amid the ruins of the Roman fort. In medieval times the site was used as a quarry for Cockermouth Castle. In modern times old peoples' bungalows have been built across part of the site.

**Aerial photograph of Old Carlisle, near Wigton.**

# *Windermere to the Sea*

THREE forts are known along the impressively-engineered Roman road from Ravenglass on the coast over Hardknott and Wrynose passes to Ambleside fort at the head of Windermere. This was the famous Tenth Iter of the Antonine Itinerary, the only point south of Carlisle where it recorded a route across Cumbria.

**Ravenglass.**

It is difficult to detect marks of the Romans occupation at Ravenglass. Most people know the village best as the start of the Ravenglass-Eskdale miniature railway. The site of a Roman fort lies south of the village, between the rivers Mite and Esk, but it is covered by a plantation and is bisected by the railway. If a visitor, descending from A595 towards the village, takes the first lane on the left through the white gates he will soon reach the ruined shell of "Walls Castle", the remains of the fort bath house.

The Roman masonry is still standing twelve feet high. Once hidden by vegetation, the site has been cleared and exposed within a neat fencing. We can pick out doorways leading into several rooms and also wall niches. The bath house has never been excavated. Collingwood argued for an Agricolan fort at Ravenglass in 1927 and placed Agricola's intended Irish expedition here. The second proposition is rejected today in favour of S.W. Scotland. A local antiquary the late Miss M. C. Fair, recorded finds from the area, such as pottery and coins

The four-acre fort faced up Eskdale. Here was the start of the Tenth Iter and one would expect a port while placenames in the local fields suggest a large *vicus*. There is Flavian pottery from Ravenglass but the first stone fort would be Trajanic or Hadrianic, with an occupation lasting into the late fourth century, the only known garrison being an infantry unit, Coh.I Morinorum. The fort's Roman name was Glannaventa, "the town on the bank," a hint of the Roman fort and civil settlement which grew up in the area of the natural harbours formed by the confluence of the rivers Mite, Irt and Esk.

If the visitor is disappointed with Ravenglass he must return to A595 and travel towards Holmrook. On the left in the distance are the towers of Calder Hall Power Station, symbols of the twentieth century; to the right lies a panoramic grouping of the Cumbrian fells.

The next Roman fort lies at Hardknott, nine miles N.E. of Ravenglass. The site is reached from Holmrook up Eskdale; in summer a pleasant alternative route is to travel on the miniature railway from Ravenglass to Dalegarth station, and then walk up the valley, returning for the evening train back to Ravenglass.

### Hardknott Castle.

This is the best-preserved Roman fort in Cumberland south of Hadrian's Wall and also one of the most outstanding remains of the Roman army in Britain. The fort was built in the early second century under Trajan and finished under the Emperor Hadrian, whose name and titles occur on a fragmentary gateway inscription found near the east gate in 1964. Its Hadrianic garrison was the 4th cohort of Delmatians. The fort was probably evacuated during the reign of Antoninus Pius but reoccupied in the 160s under the governor Sextus Calpurnius Agricola, whose name may occur on another inscription found at Hardknott in 1855. The fort was sacked in 197 and never reoccupied. It thus had a short life compared with its sister forts along the road.

The site was first mentioned by Camden in 1607 but was not identified as a Roman fort until 1694, when the Leeds antiquary, Ralph Thoresby, saw it on his way from Kendal to the coast. The first plan, of 1792, was published with a description in Hutchinson's *History of Cumberland* in 1794.

Hardknott fort was excavated between 1889 and 1894, the Ministry of Works acquiring the site in the 1950s. It was cleared and solidified. Here is a small three acre stone auxiliary fort, an external bath house and a parade ground lying near the Ravenglass-Ambleside road. There are two car parks for visitors.

The fort was built on the only available spur beneath the summit of Hardknott Fell. From the top of the Pass both the fort and the sea can be observed on a clear day. Wordsworth mentions the site in his Duddon sonnets of 1820, writing about "that lone camp on Hardknott's height whose guardians bend the knee to Jove and Mars." The Roman name was Mediobogdum, "the fort in the middle of the curve," a reference to its position in relation to the Esk below.

Visitors can reach the fort by a track skirting the external bath house, whose rooms are neatly labelled. The building (*balneum*) consisted of a stokehole and three rooms of graded temperature, heated by an underfloor hypocaust or central heating system. Notice the cold plunge bath in the last changing room. Outside was a circular heated room, a *laconicum*, which had a domed roof and its own stokehole.

Continuing up the path we see the fort walls, a notice by the south gate stating that the walls above the slate line are rebuilt from fallen masonry. The fort wall, made of local stone, had an earth bank behind it. In each corner are the foundations of the stone angle towers. The four gaps in each straight side of the walls mark the gates. All except the north gate, which overlooks a precipice, have a double portal. The gates are unlike those of the Wall forts and lack guard chambers. Two wooden doors were fitted on either side of the arched gateway and still to be seen at the west gate is one of the pivot holes on which the gate swung. Blocks of Cumberland red sandstone lying around the site must have been brought to the fort from outcrops on the coast.

Beyond the single-portalled north gate is the edge of the cliff, and an outstanding view of the Esk and the Scafell range. The cliff edge point is thus a place where a visitor might sit down and think of the motives that brought the Romans to this remote spot. Back in the fort the knoll on which the N.E. angle tower sits should be climbed for an overall view of the camp and the exposed central buildings, the commander's house (unfinished), headquarters and granary. The back and front of the fort, now overgrown with grass, would have contained the barracks. Two fine Roman shoes were found in excavations north of the granary. Other finds within the fort include pieces of Samian and coarse pottery, glass ware, brooches, beads, rings, a lead sling-bullet and pioneer axe-sheath, coins, whetstones, nails, spear heads and fragments of a soldiers leather tunic.

47

Above: The fort site from Hardknott Pass.

THE FOR

Below: South gate, looking towards the Pass.

Above: Bath House outside the South Gate.

**DKNOTT**

Below: The fort as seen from Harter Fell.

The headquarters building is of a common plan with two L-shaped rooms flanking the entrance, the cross hall without the customary tribunal and three rooms at the back, the central room being the regimental chapel or *aedes*. The granary can be identified by its heavily-buttressed walls and the foundations of two loading platforms for moving supplies into and out of the building facing the fort cross street. The commander's house towards the west gate was never finished, consisting only of an "L" shaped block. A walk of 250 yards from the fort's east gate, terminates at the parade ground (*campus*). Hardknott has the best preserved Roman fort parade ground visible in Britain. It is slightly larger in area than the fort and was artificially levelled and embanked below the mountain, being known in the 19th century as the "bowling green." On its north side is a long grass-grown ramp which led to the tribunal or review stand platform, used by the officer conducting the exercises.

Most visitors to Hardknott have been impressed by the site and its setting. R. S. Ferguson, writing in 1892, called it "an enchanting fortress in the air." The novelist Hugh Walpole in *Katherine Christian,* makes Nicholas stand here and ponder the significance of these ruined walls among the remote hills, "a fortress . . so strong that the skeleton of it would last forever, so beautiful because all around it are some of the greatest mountains of Cumberland, built by the Romans—the only power that subdued the savage north." Nicholas imagined the troops stationed here, the clang of their harness and the trumpets echoing over Harter Fell.

A visitor might cross the road, scale the cleft of Hardknott gill and reach the fellside opposite the fort, to look over the site. Artists, following Collingwood, have tried to recreate the scene in Roman times—the tree felling, scrub and rock clearance, erection of the fort walls, tooling of the sandstone, raising of the gates and towers. It is not difficult to visualise the Roman auxiliary soldiers on duty here, the rumble of creaking ox waggons up the pass, or the glint of metal on the parade ground, strange voices and the harsh din of bugles.

Leaving the site we travel up over the Pass making for Ambleside via Wrynose.

**Ambleside.**

Ambleside Roman fort is disappointing after Hardknott. The site, at Borrans, Waterhead, in low lying fields at the end of Windermere, is unimpressive and neglected. The modern road skirts the site and travellers heading for the Langdales probably do not appreciate the significance of the pens surrounding the fort gates, corner towers and central range of buildings. R. G. Collingwood excavated the site before and during World War I and uncovered the buildings of the visible stone fort. He claimed to have also detected an earlier turf and timber fort partly buried beneath the present one, which he attributed to Agricola.

The first stone Trajanic-Hadrianic fort was protected on the west by the river Rothay and the lake where there were dock facilities. The east gate has double portal guard chambers but the rest are single portal. In the middle of the fort lie the Commander's House, Headquarters and granaries. Notice the HQ courtyard and the tribunal or officer's stand at the end of the cross hall. The back room or chapel (*aedes*), contained an underground strong room for the garrison pay chests. The granaries are heavily buttressed and have long narrow sill walls inside the building to allow air to circulate and to discourage damp and vermin. The grassy parts of the fort containing the troop barracks have not been excavated.

Forts like Ambleside were held by auxiliaries. Such troops wore body armour, leather jerkins and metal helmets, and carried circular shields, with a sword and dagger hanging from a belt. They wore leather half-trousers and military boots. Some units had archers and slingers while auxiliary cavalry units rode gaily decorated steeds and had special parade armour.

The finds from Collingwood's excavations here, together with models of the forts, can be seen in the Armitt Library Museum in Ambleside. The fort had the usual external village and a tombstone found here in 1963 mentions a 35 year old record clerk, Flavius Romanus, who was killed by the enemy. Pottery and coins suggest an occupation deep into the 4th century.

The fort was then called Galava, the present name "Borrans" being Norse and meaning a "heap of stones," perhaps an indication that the fort was in ruins when it was given its new name.

# Forts of the North-West

**Lancaster.**

Lancaster with its new University, flats and urban development is a fast changing city. Its place name betrays its Roman origin although the fort name is unknown and there is little visible of Roman Lancaster. The hill top above the river Lune is now dominated by the battlemented castle and St. Marys Parish Church, but Professor Richmond's excavations established structural evidence for a succession of forts on and around the hill, the first being Agricolan, the last a Saxon Shore type fort. New excavations have begun.

Lancaster City museum, in Market Square, contains an interesting selection of Roman pottery and inscriptions from the area about the fort, and there are several milestones from the approach roads. Roman roads led northwards towards Watercrook and eastwards along the Lune valley where Caton has produced a Hadrianic milestone. It is easy to imagine the first Roman settlement on the hilltop, a fort with a sprawling village beneath and docks on the Lune crowded with galleys.

Leaving Lancaster follow A683 along the Lune valley to the next fort at Burrow. Along our way there are a fine series of motte and bailey castles to be seen at Caton, Hornby, Melling and Burton in Lonsdale—relics of later Medieval lords who, like the Romans, firmly established their presence in Lunesdale.

**Burrow-in-Lonsdale.**

Burrow-in-Lonsdale is a tiny sleepy village overlooking the broad flat meadows of the Lune valley. At the north end of the village rises the impressive Georgian facade of Burrow

**Roman milestone near Middleton Church, upper Lunesdale.**

Hall. The Roman forts lie buried here, in the fields and under the house and farm buildings. Excavations by the late O. H. North and E. J. W. Hildyard established four fort periods, from Agricola till the fourth century but Camden first mentions the site and early visitors record traces of a large village outside the fort spreading down to the river. Burrow's Roman name was "Galacum," "The Noisy One," perhaps an equation of the nearby Leck beck with a similar torrent in Southern Italy.

Four Roman inscriptions have been found in the area; an altar to the god Contrebis by a civilian, a family tombstone from Tunstall, an altar to Apollo from Kirkby Lonsdale and a dedication by a Roman doctor to the patron deity of the medical profession. Leaving the village we continue along A683 for two miles towards Kirkby Lonsdale, turn right towards Sedbergh past the fine Devil's Bridge and make for Middleton church. Here a Roman milestone stands in a field above Middleton church. Its tall shaft can be seen beneath a clump of trees. Found in 1837, it was re-erected near the passing Roman Ribchester-Carlisle road and bears the Latin numerals 53, the distance from here to Roman Carlisle.

## Watercrook.

Modern Kendal lies in a dell with a backcloth of hills. The town is the gateway to the Lake District, famous for shoes, mint cake and its ruined castle, where Henry VIII's last wife was born. Approaching on the A65, turn left at Kendal Grammar School down a branch road to Natland. After $\frac{1}{4}$ mile fork right down a narrow lane to Watercrook farm by the shoe factory. The Roman fort and *vicus* lie buried in flat fields between the farm and the river Kent which encircles the site. The Fort platform is just visible.

Excavations in 1930 and 1944 revealed the 4 acre stone fort of Alauna. Finds indicate an occupation from Agricola till the late 4th century, and these can be seen in Kendal museum near the station. A Roman altar, found recently in the river bank, was put on exhibition in the factory.

The main North-South Ribchester to Carlisle road which skirts the Lake District on the east was protected by forts at Low Borrow Bridge, Brougham and Old Penrith. At Brougham the road was joined by the Stainmore Pass route with its own forts at Kirkby Thore, Brough under Stainmore, Bowes and Greta Bridge.

## Low Borrow Bridge.

The fort at Low Borrow Bridge near Tebay can be reached from Kendal on A685. Its site is hidden from view in a field behind some cottages by the bridge carrying the railway at Castlehows. The first fort to be dug by the Cumberland and Westmorland Archaeological Society, this is an isolated fort and is not mentioned by Leland, Camden or Horsley. The first reference to it comes from 1777 when it was described as a castle.

In 1812 it was recognised as a Roman fort and in 1827 John Just, a schoolmaster from Kirkby Lonsdale, reported that the site was being used as a quarry by local farmers. There have been minor excavations in 1883, the early 1930s and in 1952. The Fort platform is still clear but the first fort was probably built under Agricola. It housed an infantry battalion of 500 men in three acres, and, it can be seen from the Kendal approach road that the fort occupies a striking position in the Lune gorge, hemmed in by mountains on all sides.

Roads led from it to Watercrook and maybe to Brough via Crosby Garrett. The fort's function was obviously to keep the Lune valley route open. From Tebay it is possible to go via Orton to Crosby Ravensworth village and see Ewe Close and the native settlements on Crosby Ravensworth fell.

**Brougham.**

Brougham fort can be seen at Eamont Bridge on the A6 1½ miles south of Penrith. The Roman fort of Brocavum lies near the castle in a field by the river Eamont. The fort, astride the trunk route, was an important road centre, east over Stainmore, southwards over Shap and north to Carlisle. Here began the branch route to Ambleside, the famous High Street, a "must" for the historically minded walker.

Twenty or more inscriptions have been found in the fort area mentioning Jupiter, Mars and Belatucadrus. Tombstones

**The fort at Brougham in the Eden Valley.**

testify to a thriving *vicus* whose cemetery, beside the Stainmore road, has recently been excavated. The fort, founded by Agricola, was occupied until the late fourth century and its cavalry garrison was responsible for keeping the surrounding routes open to travellers. The survival of the Roman place name and the missionary work of Ninian in the district suggest the continuing into sub-Roman times of a sizable population in the vicinity of the fort.

### Old Penrith.

Old Penrith fort, Voreda, is four miles north of modern Penrith and 13 miles south of Carlisle. It is reached along A6, a mile north of Plumpton Wall at Castlesteads. The fort platform, which lies in the fields by the river Petteril, is an oft forgotten site, and has never been excavated. There have been many inscriptions found, dedicated to deities such as Jupiter, Mars, Mercury, Venus, the Mother Goddesses, Silvanus and Belatucadrus. Occupation is attested from Hadrian until the fourth century; tombstones indicate that there was a *vicus* outside the fort. The 2nd cohort of Gauls was in garrison during the third century. Voreda was a route hub with roads to the Wall, Old Carlisle and Keswick.

## THE STAINMORE PASS FORTS.

### Kirkby Thore.

Kirkby Thore village lies five miles north of Appleby and can be reached from Brougham along A66. The Roman fort is buried North-East of the village and the main road, in fields above the river Troutbeck. Its defences show up clearly on air photographs. Between the fort and Piper lane was a large 30 acre civil settlement which grew up into a walled town. The fort name was Bravoniacum—"Place of Querns" and it lay on the north side of the Roman road from York, at the point where the Maiden Way Roman road leaves it to give access to the lead mining area around Alston.

Kirkby Thore fort was a checkpoint and depot for the lead coming south and inscriptions tell of a long occupation from Agricola till the late fourth century. The existence of a third century cavalry unit is proved by the tombstone of a retired officer who died in Algeria and whose family remembered his service at Bravoniacum, in distant Britain beneath the leaden skies of Stainmore.

The fort site on Burwens hill was looted for building the village and part of the fort lies under the road and modern

OLD PENRITH FORT BESIDE THE A.6
NORTH OF THE PRESENT TOWN.

KIRKBY THORE FORT AS SEEN FROM THE AIR.

houses. There are records of antiquities being found here since the 17th century. The last excavations were in 1961. From Kirkby Thore to Brough and on over the pass to Bowes the Roman road was guarded by fortlets and signal stations.

### Whitley Castle.

From Kirkby Thore a Roman road—the Maiden Way—led to the Wall via the fort at Whitley Castle outside Alston.

The highest market town in England, Alston, can be reached along A686 from Eamont Bridge and Langwathby, a solitary route over the fells. The fort lies five miles north of Alston off B6295 on Whitley Common, and is just in Northumberland. It is well worth the detour. The fort platform is defended by an impressive series of ditches protecting it on all four sides but with a concentration on the uphillside, with seven ditches in 150 feet, at the point where the enemy might be tempted to charge the defences. These are the best preserved Roman fort ditches in Britain after Ardoch fort in Perthshire. The fort is of an unusual rhomboid shape instead of the normal rectangle. The second cohort of Nervians made up the fort garrison and protected the Maiden Way and the nearby lead deposits.

### Brough under Stainmore.

To find the site of the Roman fort at Brough in Westmorland one must first find the castle situated on a brow in Church Brough overlooking the Swindale Beck. The Norman castle builders erected their castle in the northern half of the deserted Roman fort.

Brough fort held 500 men and was connected to the passing Stainmore cross route. The fort itself faced south, turning its back on the Roman road, and its function was to guard the western end of the Stainmore Pass and police southwards through Ravenstonedale and Mallerstang. Its Roman name was Verterae, "summit," an apt description of its position above the beck, and from within the castle courtyard there is a good view of the surrounding district.

Brough has produced two inscriptions found built into the nearby church of St Michael, a late second century Severan building inscription and a tombstone of a sixteen year old lad written in Greek; Hermes from Commagene, perhaps the son of a local trader. The site has yielded many lead seals and was a mining depot. Leave the castle and return to Market Brough; join the Stainmore Pass route and make for Bowes twelve miles eastwards.

WHITLEY CASTLE, NEAR ALSTON

*This high Pennine fort is famous for its series of
well-preserved ditches, which protected the fort
enclosure.*

The Stainmore Pass route is very historic and has seen many travellers from Bronze Age smiths to commercial waggons. The Romans built three forts along it and were the first to lay a road across it. Medieval Kings followed with a line of castles. Three Roman signal posts are known along the pass at Maiden Castle (five miles east of Brough), Roper Castle (one and a half miles south-west of Maiden Castle) and at Bowes Moor opposite the hotel. These can be visited on foot but you will need the relevant one-inch Ordnance Survey Sheet.

On the summit of the pass the earth ramparts of Rey Cross Roman marching camp can be seen silhouetted against the sky-

**Brough-under-Stainmore, showing the medieval castle built within the Roman fort enclosure.**

**Bronze statuette of a dog from Kirkby Thore.**

line. The Roman road cuts straight through, obliterating two of its gates, so the camp is earlier than the road. It once accommodated a Legion in its $18\frac{1}{2}$ acres. Notice the gate gaps and the outer obstacle *titulus* or mound. Here on this desolate summit it is easy to imagine a tented army poised for the early exploration of Cumbria. Today traffic roars through the camp, oblivious of its existence.

In the field opposite Bowes Moor hotel is the small Roman signal post and towards Bowes the squat medieval castle keep comes into view.

### Bowes.

Lavatrae Roman fort is largely covered by the village of Bowes, St. Giles Church, vicarage and castle. There is a fine Severan building inscription in the church chancel. The camp lay on a hill top above the river Greta where its southern platform can be seen below the castle, and the bath house was between the fort and the river. Its Roman name means "Riverbed". A Hadrianic building inscription from the fort mentions the governor Sextus Julius Severus (130 to 133) while two altars from Bowes moor record dedications to the hunting god Silvanus. Excavations to uncover the fort headquarters and granary took place in the summer of 1970.

Leaving Bowes continue to Greta Bridge. The Roman fort here lies in a field behind the hotel. It has produced a Severan building inscription (now in Bowes Museum) recording the recovery of the Stainmore route after the disaster of 197.

# Continued Research

IN this final chapter some of the unresolved problems of Roman Cumbria must be considered. We still know very little about the early local campaigns of Cerialis and Agricola and have much pottery but little structural evidence of the Agricolan forts. In the north more is being discovered about the Stanegate Frontier, and a new fort site has been identified at Kirkbride, south of Bowness. Work continues along Hadrian's Wall and the researches of Mr. R. L. Bellhouse into the Hadrianic Cumberland coastal defences will eventually enable a detailed account of the whole system to be produced. All the forts in the hinterland deserve individual studies of the type made by Professor Birley.

More excavation is needed, for some of the forts have never been dug scientifically, and there is no full plan of any fort in the Lake Counties. Questions still abound. How, for instance did fort plans change in Roman times? Which forts were held late? What was the purpose of individual forts like Caermote? Is there a lost fort site at or near Keswick, as is implied by the road system? Excavation may produce new inscriptions telling us about units in garrison. Altars may still be buried in pits around the Hardknott parade ground, as one 19th century visitor suggested. The extra-mural *vici* also need more study. We know little about their development, plans and buildings. The Roman road network in the area has still not been fully elucidated.

The road system around forts like Lancaster, Burrow, Watercrook, and Low Borrow Bridge needs clarifying, perhaps by locally-based field workers. There may have been a Roman route through Furness. How widespread were the native sites? Did the Romans encourage native agriculture in the hinterland of Hadrian's Wall and are there regional differences in the types of settlement? What we need is much more evidence from native sites to substantiate the notion that there was a large native population. More might be discovered about the towns of Carlisle and Kirkby Thore, the type of buildings Roman Luguvalium contained and the administrative importance it attained. Are there no villa sites in the Cumberland Plain?

Little is known about industrial exploitation, the lead mining around Alston or the industrial activities of the workshops in some of the *vici*. More fort and *vicus* excavation might reveal more evidence of the official cults in the Roman army and about local gods. Were there any Mithraic temples outside our forts? Analogy with other provinces can tell us something about everyday life and dress, but the questions continue. What did the citizens of Roman Carlisle or the villagers of Ewe Close wear? Did Roman soldiers' dress and equipment change much in Roman times? What transport vehicles can we envisage trundling up Eskdale or in convoy over Stainmore? What use did the Romans make of sea and river transport?

The accepted history of chronological events needs re-examination. In times of revolt and incursion from the North, were the Brigantes always involved? How far did the northern tribes penetrate in 197, 296 and 367; was their damage local or widespread; did some forts escape unscathed; and what were the late-Roman military dispositions in NW England? Was the western coast above and below Lancaster equipped with a signalling system? In another realm of inquiry we need to know more about when Roman troops finally left our district, and what became of the sub-Roman inhabitants? Was there continuity of life in towns such as Carlisle?

These are some of the questions the interested amateur might ask professional archaeologists working on Roman sites in the Lake Counties. They and their successors will painstakingly reassemble the faded jigsaw puzzle of the past.

A **trumpet brooch** from Stanwix, near Carlisle.

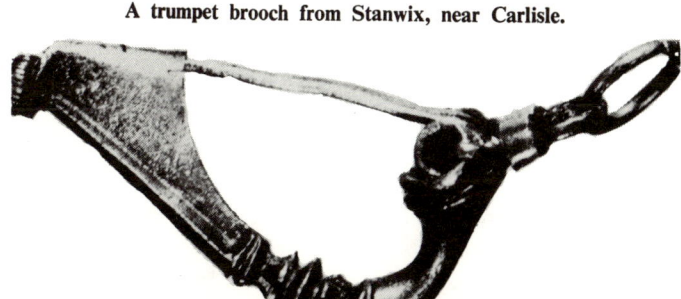

# ADDENDUM TO THIRD EDITION

I HAVE taken the opportunity of a third edition to correct some errors, indicate new discoveries and provide additional notes and references.

Many archaeologists now think Hadrian's Wall and its hinterland forts were damaged in AD 180 rather than in 197 (pages 14, 19, 46 and 65). A new Department of Classics and Archaeology has been established at Lancaster University. A survey of all post-war excavations on Roman Lancaster is to be published in 1976 (page 52). It has been suggested that the Roman name for the Lune valley was Contrebis. Excavations by Lancaster University began at Watercrook in 1974 (page 54). A new chronology was established in 1974/5. The first fort was built after Agricola in the 90s, the last abandoned about 340. The new finds can be seen in Kendal Museum. There is an interesting account of the Roman fort by the 17th century antiquary Thomas Machell. A small Roman site has been postulated, on pottery evidence, at Hincaster, south of Kendal. A new three acre Roman fort was identified and excavated at Troutbeck in 1974, nine miles east of Keswick (page 56). A rescue operation was carried out by Lancaster University at Bowness on Solway fort in 1971 (CW2, 1975), pages 33 and 36.

Air photography and fieldwork has revealed extensive native sites and field systems in the area of Crosby Ravensworth, Crosby Garrett and Waitby in the Kirkby Stephen area (pages 14, 22, 28, 55). Air photography by Manchester University in the extremely dry summer of 1975 revealed some 150 new native farmsteads on the Cumberland Plain (pages 42-3) and that the Roman Cumberland coastal defences in the area of the Solway Firth had defensive ditches and an anti-personnel stake line (Illustrated London News, January 1976, page 19). Bigland's milefortlet I was excavated by Lancaster University. Excavations at Carlisle (page 42) failed to locate the Roman town wall (Britannia V, 1974, pages 410-11). Excavations on the Roman tilery at Scalesceugh south-east of Carlisle continued in 1971/2.

Ambleside Roman fort site is to be transferred by the National Trust to the Department of the Environment for consolidation (page 51). Collingwood's finds of 1914-20 can now be seen in the library of Brockhole National Park Centre between Ambleside and Windermere. A new Dalesman minibook guide to the fort was published in 1975. The first fort was post Agricolan built in the 90s; the last stone fort abandoned in AD 383. A research thesis on the fort by R. Copping of

Kendal can be studied in Ambleside library.

Hardknott was a new stone Hadrianic fort (page 46). The new inscription can be seen in Tullie House Museum, Carlisle. Numerous leather military shoes, tent and shield cover fragments, found by Miss Charlesworth, are reported in Britannia IV, 1973. A small latrine building was identified near the fort's south-west angle tower in 1975. Note the Roman drain running across the fort, its entry visible outside the north-east angle tower. The red sandstone blocks outside the fort came from Gosforth or St. Bees. The fort is now signposted by the bath house. A new survey of Roman Ravenglass was published by R. Copping in 1976. The fort bath house (page 45) was first excavated in 1881 by William Jackson. It too is now signposted. Visitors to Ravenglass should not miss seeing the fine reconstruction painting of Hardknott Roman fort by W. G. Collingwood made in 1894. It can be seen in Muncaster Castle. Fieldwork has established a probable Roman route through Furness, south of Ravenglass. To reach Maryport Roman fort (page 40), follow camp street from the market place. The Maryport Roman altars are still not available for public view.

Excavations in 1971/2 examined a Roman cremation cemetery east of Brough fort (page 59). To find the Roman signal stations along the Stainmore Pass (pages 62-3), follow the map instructions in Roger Wilson's "Roman Remains in Britain", pages 222-4 (see below). Two new signal stations have been found on the Pass. Air photographs show clearly a large vicus outside Old Carlisle Fort—including a mansio (pages 43-4). It is clear that Roman Cumbria had a very large native population (page 23). An aqueduct channel supplying Bowes Roman fort has been plotted (YAJ, pages 181-4, 1973). The village outside Greta Bridge fort (page 63) has been examined by excavation. On Hadrian's Wall new sections of curtain wall can now be seen at Gilsland and on both sides of Birdoswald fort (pages 33-4).

A new important report was published by Professor Anne Robertson in 1975 on Birrens Roman fort (map, page 8). A full bibliography of Professor Eric Birley's articles on Roman sites in Cumbria, 1928 - 1974, was published in Britannia VI, pages xi - xxviii, 1975, to mark his 70th birthday. To locate Roman sites on the ground in Cumbria the best book published recently is "A Guide to the Roman Remains in Britain", R. J. A. Wilson, Constable 1974. There are now two guide books to Hardknott Roman fort, a Dalesman mini-book (3rd edition, 1975) and a larger photographic study published in 1974. A new Penguin paperback by Dobson and Breeze on

Hadrian's Wall, presenting new theories on its chronology, is due for publication in 1976. Two other recently published works are "The Armour of Imperial Rome", H. R. Robinson, Arms-Armour Press 1975; and "The Roman Army", P. Connolly, Macdonald 1975.

Finally, it is necessary to correct or amplify certain statements in the existing text. The following lines should read as follows:- Page 20, last line: "smoke not semaphore signals". Page 27, 2nd paragraph, penultimate line: "in the fourth century . . . " Page 28, 2nd paragraph, line 7: "the odd pieces of chain mail . . . " Page 45, **Ravenglass,** 1st paragraph, line 7: "through the open gates . . . "; 2nd paragraph, line 4: "several rooms and also wall niche. The bath house has once . . . " Page 46, **Hardknott Castle,** 1st paragraph, line 4: "the early second century in stone . . . " Page 50, 2nd paragraph, line 3: "an enchanted fortress . . . " Page 63, line 4, and page 73: Titulum.

# Reference Section

## A SELECT LIST OF ROMAN EMPERORS

**Julio-Claudians.  31  B.C. — 68 A.D.**
| | |
|---|---|
| Augustus | 31 B.C. — 14 A.D. |
| Tiberius | 14 — 37 |
| Gaius (Caligula) | 37 — 41 |
| Claudius | 41 — 54 |
| Nero | 54 — 68 |
| Galba, Otho, Vitellius | 68 — 69 |

**Flavians     69  A.D. — 96  A.D.**
| | |
|---|---|
| Vespasian | 69 — 79 |
| Titus | 79 — 81 |
| Domitian | 81 — 96 |

**"Adoptive Emperors" 96 A.D.—138 A.D.**
| | |
|---|---|
| Nerva | 96 — 98 |
| Trajan | 98 — 117 |
| Hadrian | 117 — 138 |

**Antonines     138 A.D. — 192 A.D.**
| | |
|---|---|
| Antoninus Pius | 138 — 161 |
| Marcus Aurelius | 161 — 180 |
| Commodus | 180 — 192 |
| Pertinax, Didius Julianus | 193 |

**Severans     193 A.D. — 235 A.D.**
| | |
|---|---|
| Septimius Severus | 193 — 211 |
| Caracalla | 212 — 217 |
| Macrinus | 217 — 218 |
| Elagabalus | 218 — 222 |
| Severus Alexander | 222 — 235 |

**Later  Emperors.**
| | |
|---|---|
| Gordian III | 238 — 244 |
| Diocletian | 284 — 305 |
| Constantine | 307 — 337 |
| Valentinian | 364 — 375 |
| Honorius | 395 — 423 |

# CHRONOLOGICAL TABLE OF EVENTS IN ROMAN BRITAIN

**A.D.**

| | |
|---|---|
| 43 | Romans invade Southern Britain. |
| 43 — 50 | Conquest of the South. Brigantes become Client-Kingdom allied to Rome. |
| 68 — 69 | Brigantes break with Rome. |
| 71 — 74 | Cerialis defeats Brigantes |
| 79 — 84 | Agricola campaigns in Northern Britain. |
| 122 | Hadrian visits Britain. |
| 120 — 138 | Hadrian's frontier wall built. |
| 139 — 143 | Romans invade Scotland. Antonine Wall built. |
| 155 — 159 | Romans re-occupy Pennines. Julius Verus Governor. |
| 163 — 166 | Calpurnius Agricola Governor. |
| 193 — 197 | Clodius Albinus, Governor of Britain, invades Continent. Is defeated and killed near Lyons in Gaul by Severus. |
| 197 — 208 | Northern tribes break through Hadrian's Wall. Severus' governors recover Wall and Hinterland forts. |
| 208 — 211 | Severus in Britain. Invasion of Caledonia. |
| 211 | Severus dies at York. |
| 286 — 296 | Usurpation of Carausius and Allectus. |
| 296 | Allectus defeated by Constantius. Northern tribes break through Hadrian's Wall. |
| 296 — 306 | Constantius I recovers North. |
| 306 | Constantius I dies at York. |
| 367 | Picts, Scots and Attacotti break through Wall. |
| 367 — 369 | Valentinian sends Theodosius to expel invaders. |
| 383 — 388 | Usurpation of Magnus Maximus. |
| 407 — 411 | Constantine III, usurper, withdraws troops. |
| 410 | Honorius instructs Britain to provide for its own defences against invaders. |

# LIST OF ROMAN FORT NAMES

**Hadrian's wall and its Outpost Forts.**
Birdoswald—CAMBOGLANNA.
Bewcastle—FANUM COCIDI
Netherby—CASTRA EXPLORATORVM
Castlesteads—UXELLODUNVM.
Stanwix—PETRIANA.
Burgh-by-Sands—ABALLAVA.
Drumburgh—CONGAVATA.
Bowness—MAIA.

**Cumberland Coastal Defences.**
Beckfoot—BIBRA.
Maryport—ALAUNA.
Burrow Walls—GABROSENTUM.
Moresby—TUNNOCELUM.

**Cumberland Plain.**
Carlisle—LUGUVALIUM.
Old Carlisle—OLENACUM.
Caermote—?
Papcastle—DERVENTIO.

**The Lakes.**
Ravenglass—GLANNAVENTA.
Hardknott—MEDIOBOGDUM.
Ambleside—GALAVA.

**North West.**
Lancaster—?
Burrow—GALACUM.
Watercrook—ALAUNA.

**Eastern Forts.**
Old Penrith—VOREDA.
Brougham—BROCAVUM.
Kirkby Thore—BRAVONIACUM.
Whitley Castle—?
Brough-under-Stainmore—VERTERAE.
Bowes—LAVATRAE.
Greta Bridge—MAGLONA.
Low Borrow Bridge—?

BIRDOSWALD FORT ON HADRIAN'S WALL
(A RECONSTRUCTION BY ALAN SORRELL)

# A GLOSSARY

ALA. An auxiliary cavalry unit of the Roman Imperial Army.

AUXILIA. Battalions of 500 and 1,000 infantry or cavalry stationed in forts.

BALNEUM. Military bath house outside a fort.

BASILICA. Roman town hall; cross hall of a Fort HQ.

BELATUCADRUS. Local god equated with Mars.

BELLONA. Goddess of war.

BRIGANTIA—Tribal realm of the Brigantes in Northern England.

CAMPUS. Parade ground outside a fort.

CIVITAS. Tribal unit.

COCIDIUS. Local god equated with Mars worshipped in Cumberland.

COHORT. Infantry regiment of 500 or 1,000 troops quartered in a fort.

CONTREBIS. Local godling worshipped at Burrow in Lancashire.

CHI-RHO. Monogram of Christ.

FORUM. Market square in a Roman town.

HORREA. Granaries inside a Roman fort.

JUPITER. Jupiter Best and Greatest, chief god of the Roman state.

LEGION. Unit of the Roman army, nominally 6.000 strong, based in a legionary fortress.

MARS. Roman war god.

MERCURY. Roman god of trade.

MITHRAISM. Eastern mystery religion based upon worship of god Mithras in a special temple (mithraeum), outside the fort or in a town.

PRAEFECTUS COHORTIS. Auxiliary infantry unit commander.

PRAETENTURA. Interior of a Roman fort lying in front of the via principalis and containing the barracks.

PRINCIPIA. The Headquarters building in the centre of a Roman fort.

PRAETORIUM. The Commander's House inside a Roman fort.

RETENTURA. The interior of a Roman fort that lies behind the Headquarters building.

SAMIAN WARE. Roman best table pottery with a glossy red surface, manufactured in Gaul, imported into Britain.

SILVANUS. Local god of woodland and hunting.

TITULUS. A detached length of bank and ditch covering the entrance gate of a Roman marching camp to break up an attack.

TRIBUNAL. A platform in the hall of the Headquarters Building of a fort on which the commanding officer of the garrison took his seat on ceremonial or official occasions; also a parade ground platform outside the fort.

VALLUM. The earthwork ditch system dug behind Hadrian's Wall.

VIA PRINCIPALIS. Main cross street inside a Roman fort joining the two lateral gates.

VICANI. Villagers.

VICUS. Village that grew up outside a Roman fort.

VILLA. Romanised farm house, buildings and estate.

VINOTONUS. Local stream god equated with Silvanus.

VULCAN. Roman god of Fire.

## SOME ROMAN GOVERNORS OF BRITAIN.

A.D.

| | |
|---|---|
| Aulus Plautius | 43–47 |
| P. Ostorius Scapula | 47–52 |
| A. Didius Gallus | 52–57 |
| Q. Veranius | 57–58 |
| G. Suetonius Paulinus | 58–61 |
| G. Petronius Turpilianus | 61–63 |
| M. Trebellius Maximus | 63–69 |
| M. Vettius Bolanus | 69–71 |
| Q. Petillius Cerialis | 71–74 |
| Sex. Julius Frontinus | 74–78 |
| Gn. Julius Agricola | 78–85 |
| Q. Pompeius Falco | 118–122 |
| A. Platorius Nepos | 122–124 |
| Sex. Julius Severus | 130–133 |
| P. Mummius Sisenna | 135– |
| Q. Lollius Urbicus | 139–142 |
| Cn. Julius Verus | 155–158 |
| M. Statius Priscus | 161–162 |
| Sex. Calpurnius Agricola | 162–165 |
| D. Clodius Albinus | 192–197 |
| Virius Lupus | 197–202 |
| C. Valerius Pudens | 202–205 |
| L. Alfenus Senecio | 205–207 |

# BIBLIOGRAPHY

**1. General works.**

*Birley, A.*—Life in Roman Britain, London 1964.
    —Hadrian's Wall. An illustrated Guide, H.M.S.O 1963.

*Birley, E.*—Research on Hadrian's Wall, Kendal 1961.
    —"The Hinterland of Hadrian's Wall," Transactions A.A.S.D. & N, xl (1958).

*Bruce, J. C.*—Handbook to the Roman Wall, revised Richmond, 12th ed., Newcastle 1967.

*Collingwood and Wright*—Roman Inscriptions of Britain, Oxford 1965.

*Collingwood, R. G.*—Archaeology of Roman Britain, revised Richmond, London 1969.

*Frere, S.*—Britannia, London 1967.

*Hartley, B, R.*—"Some problems of the Roman military occupation of the North of England", Northern History, Vol. I, Leeds 1966.

*Richmond, I, A.*—Roman Britain, Penguin Books 1955.
    —(ed), Roman and Native in North Britain, Edinburgh 1958.
    —"The Roman Frontier Land," History, xliv, 1959.

*Margary, I, D.*—Roman Roads in Britain, Vol. 2, London 1957.

*RCHM*—Royal Commision on Historical Monuments: Westmorland, London 1936.

*Salway, P.*—The Frontier People of Roman Britain, Cambridge 1965.

*Toynbee, J, M, C.*—Art in Roman Britain, London 1962.

*Watson, G, R.*—The Roman Soldier, London 1969.

*Webster, G.*—The Roman Imperial Army, London 1969.

*Thomas, C.*—(ed), Rural Settlement in Roman Britain, London 1966.

*H.M. Ordnance Survey.*—A map of Roman Britain, Chessington, (3rd ed). 1956.

*H,M, Ordnance Survey.*—Map of Hadrian's Wall, Chessington, 1964.

**2. Sites.**

*Abbreviations.*

CW2—Cumberland and Westmorland Antiquarian and Archaeological Society Transactions (New Series, 1901-present). Kendal.

HSLC—Transactions of the Historic Society of Lancashire and Cheshire. Liverpool

*Bellhouse, R. L.*—Some fieldwork at Caermote, CW2 1957.
    —A Roman post at Wreay Hall near Carlisle, CW2 1953·
    —Excavations in Eskdale, the Muncaster Roman kilns, CW2 1960: 1961.
    —The Roman forts at Caermote, CW2 1960.
    —Roman sites on the Cumberland Coast, CW2 1954.
    —The Roman temporary Camps near Troutbeck, Cumberland, CW2 1956.
    —Roman sites along the Cumberland Coast 1966-67, CW2 1969; CW2 1970.

*Blake, B.*—Excavations of Native (Iron Age) sites in Cumberland, 1956-58, CW2 1959.

*Birley, E.*—Materials for the history of Roman Brougham, CW2 1932.

—Old Penrith-Voreda. CW2 1934.

—The Roman site at Burrow-in-Lonsdale, CW2 1946.

—Old Penrith and its problems, CW2 1947.

—The Roman Fort at Low Borrow Bridge, CW2 1947.

—The Roman Fort at Moresby, CW2 1948.

—The Roman Fort and Settlement at Old Carlisle, CW2 1951.

—The Roman milestone at Middleton-in-Lonsdale, CW2 1953.

—The Roman Fort at Netherby CW2 1954.

—The Roman Fort at Watercrook, CW2 1957.

—The Roman Fort at Ravenglass, CW2 1958.

—The Roman Fort at Brough-under-Stainmore, CW2 1958.

—Roman Papcastle, CW2 1963.

—Hardknott Castle Roman Fort. A bibliography of the site, CW2 1963.

*Charlesworth, D.*—Recent work at Kirkby Thore, CW2 1964.

—The Granaries at Hardknott Castle, CW2 1963.

—Excavations at Papcastle 1961-62, CW2 1965.

*Collingwood, R. G.*—Roman Eskdale, Whitehaven 1929.

—A Roman fortlet on Barrock Fell near Low Hesket, CW2 1931.

—Prehistoric settlements near Crosby Ravensworth, CW2 1933.

—Two Mountain Roads, CW2 1937.

*Hogg, R.*—Excavations of the Roman auxiliary Tilery, Brampton, CW2 1965.

*Jarrett, M. G.*—Pre-Hadrianic occupation of Roman Maryport, CW2 1958

—Roman Officers at Maryport, CW2 1965.

—"The Garrison of Maryport and the Roman Army in Britain" in *Britain and Rome,* Kendal 1966.

*Manning, W. H.*—A hoard of Romano-British iron work from Brampton, CW2 1966.

*Richmond, I. A.*—(with J. McIntyre). The Roman Camps at Rey Cross and Crackenthorpe, CW2 1934.

—Roman lead seals from Brough-under-Stainmore, CW2 1936.

—The Roman road from Ambleside to Ravenglass, CW2 1949.

—Excavations on the site of the Roman fort at Lancaster, 1950, HSLC, 1950.

—"A Roman arterial signalling system in the Stainmore Pass", in W. F. Grimes (ed), *Aspects of Archaeology in Britain and Beyond.* London, 1951.

# MILECASTLES ON HADRIAN'S WALL

Milecastle 49 and a reconstruction by Alan Sorrell of the Wall as it was carried over the River Irthing, near Birdoswald.

Model of stone wall milecastle in the Museum of Antiquities, Newcastle-upon-Tyne.

### 3. Articles

*Richmond, I. A., McIntyre, J.*—Tents of the Roman Army and leather from Birdoswald, CW2, 1934.

*Richmond, Hodgson and St. Joseph*—The Roman fort at Bewcastle, CW2, 1938.

*Richmond, I. A.*—A Roman vat of lead from Ireby Cumberland, CW2, 1945

*Hogg, R.*—A Roman cemetery site at Beckfoot, CW2, 1949.

*Hildyard and Gillam*—Renewed excavation at Low Borrow Bridge, CW2, 1951.

*Gillam, J. P.*—Calpurnius Agricola and the Northern Frontier, TDN, x, iv, 1953.

*Bellhouse, R. L.*—A newly discovered fort at Park House near Carlisle, CW2, 1954.

*Bellhouse, R. L.*—The Roman fort at Burrow Walls nr. Workington, CW2, 1955.

*Birley, E.*—The Western Sector of Hadrian's Wall, CW2, 1961.

*Bellhouse, R. L.*—Moricambe in Roman Times and Roman Sites on the Cumberland Coast, CW2, 1962.

*Birley, E., and Bellhouse, R. L.*—The Roman site at Kirkbride, CW2, 1963.

*Burkett, M. E.*—Recent discoveries at Ambleside, CW2, 1965.

*Wright, R. P.*—A Hadrianic building inscription from Hardknott, CW2, 1965.

*Bellhouse, R. L.*—The problem of Burrow Walls, CW2, 1966.

*Charlesworth, D.*—Roman leather from Hardknott, Cumberland, Ant. J., 1968.

*Davies, R. W.*—A note on Roman soldiers in quarries, CW2, 1968.

*Davies, R. W.*—Police Work in Roman Times, History Today, October, 1968.

*Jones, G. D. B.*—The Romans in the North-West, Northern History, 3, 1968.

*Howard, P.*—Birdoswald Fort on Hadrian's Wall, Cameo Books, Huddersfield, 1969.

*Davies, R. W.*—The Training Grounds of the Roman Cavalry, AJ. 1969.

*Gillam, J. P., and Mann, J. C.*—The Northern British Frontier from Antoninus Pius to Caracalla, AA, 1970.

*Davies, R. W.*—The Roman Military Diet, Britannia 2, 1971.

*Edwards, B. J. N.*—Roman finds from Contrebis, CW2, 1971.

*Bellhouse, R. L.*—The Roman Tileries at Scalesceugh and Brampton, CW2, 1971.

*Davies, R. W.*—In the Service of Rome, History Today, August, 1972.

*Hartley, B. R.*—The Roman Occupation of North Britain, Britannia 3, 1972.

*Stone head of a native God from Netherby, Cumberland.*

HARDKNOTT FORT: VIEW OF THE
NORTH WALL AND ESKDALE.